S T A Y

U N T I L

T O M O R R O W

J A C Q U E L I N E   W H I T N E Y

THOUGHT
CATALOG
Books

THOUGHTCATALOG.COM

THOUGHT
CATALOG
Books

Copyright © 2022 Jacqueline Whitney.

All rights reserved. No part of this book may be reproduced or transmitted in any
form or any means, electronic or mechanical, without prior written consent and
permission from Thought Catalog.

Published by Thought Catalog Books, an imprint of Thought Catalog, a digital
magazine owned and operated by The Thought & Expression Company LLC, an
independent media organization founded in 2010 and based in the United States of
America. For stocking inquiries, contact stockists@shopcatalog.com.

Produced by Chris Lavergne and Noelle Beams
Art direction and design by KJ Parish
Creative editorial direction by Brianna Wiest
Circulation management by Isidoros Karamitopoulos

thoughtcatalog.com | shopcatalog.com

First Edition, Limited Edition Pressing
Printed in the United States of America

ISBN 978-1-949759-50-1

I want this book to be something you can turn to when you don't feel okay, when you're tired of the fight of life and need something, literally anything, to make you feel a little bit more okay. Something to make the survival a little bit more bearable. I want it to be the comfort you need in the moments you feel lonely.

I know what it feels like to want and need it all to be over–for all of the pain to be quiet. It is a miracle that I am still here, writing these words. It is not by chance you are here, reading them. You deserve to be alive. You deserve to find the peace you need. You deserve to believe that one day soon, you can be free from the pain. Trust where you are being led to find healing. I am so thankful you are here.

This is your sign to stay another day.

Take it one tomorrow at a time.

Peace is never as far as it feels.

You deserve to see another tomorrow.

Stay.

I am so sorry you have felt the pain that you have. I am so sorry you have felt so alone and like no one understands you. I am so sorry you have felt like you don't belong here, that you aren't meant for this life. I am so sorry that you believed the only way you were going to find peace was to end your life. I am so sorry those dark thoughts ever touched your mind. I am so sorry people weren't as kind to you as you were to them. I am so sorry you were taken advantage of. I am so sorry the world became unbearable to live in. I am so sorry you know what it feels like to believe you aren't meant to be here. I hope you start to see yourself as the light that you are–you are a beacon of strength. Not just anyone could have been through what you have and still be here today living the life that you are. Even if you aren't where you want to be, you are here, filling the world with compassion. Even if you can't see your purpose clearly, you are trying, and that is enough. Your story will save someone. You are here to save people in a way no one came to save you. You are here to give hope to those who are hopeless. You will be remembered by the love you left behind. Because it's those who have been to hell and back, who have done the healing work, who have used their pain for purpose that leave the biggest impact on those they cross paths with in this life. You see, sometimes life tears our worlds apart, not because we deserve anything that happens, but because we deserve to know the beauty that always comes after pain, the power that comes from seeing yourself through what you went through. See yourself through. I promise you, one day you will look back on your life and realize that you always had what you needed to get through. If you just try to be a little less hard on yourself, you will see that at the end of the day, life is too short to live in a circle of suffering. This doesn't mean it will always be easy, but it's up to you to choose how you respond. I hope you choose to heal. I hope you choose yourself.

It is incredibly difficult to call back to trauma. It is incredibly difficult to sit with the memories of moments in your past that changed you forever. It's important to remember that what happened doesn't define who you are today. The divine strength that carried you through so that you are still here today is proof that trauma can change you, but it's not who you are. Your story isn't who you are. You are who you become from the chapters that leave you feeling broken. You can choose who you want to become. Do you want to live the rest of your life holding on to the past? Or do you want to let go of it so that you can transform your life? You are made new every day. You are given another chance every day. You deserve all of the chances you need in order to be okay.

Even after everything you have been through, you are still here. You should be so proud of how far you have come.

If your world becomes dark and nothing feels like anything anymore, I promise, you won't exist there forever. I promise, if you just try and search within yourself for any glimmer of strength you have left, and you choose to take another breath, you will find the light you need. You will find yourself looking back on these days and maybe wonder how you even came through them, how you even survived, but you will know that you would not be the person you are today without the dark days. Life isn't supposed to be a repetitive nightmare. Life is meant to be lived in love with it. You are worth living. You are still here. Thank you for being here. I am so happy you exist.

Hold on and keep holding on.

You are still loved even when you don't feel like yourself.

You are still strong even when you feel like you can't keep going.

You are still here because you are supposed to be here.

You are a light
even though the world has
been a dark place for you.
Your light is needed here.

You can't hold it in any longer. You have to pour your soul out. You have to release the deep, uncomfortable, sometimes debilitating emotions. I don't think you realize how strong you really are. You can feel painful feelings and be okay. You can let go of the attachments gripping your past. The past is over. Today is a day you've never lived before, and you can start a new story. No one is judging you as much as you judge yourself. You don't have to apologize for choosing to do what's best for you. You can step away if you need time alone, and you should never feel guilty for doing what you know is best for you at any given moment. You don't have to apologize for feeling intensely. You don't have to apologize for being emotional. Being emotional is healthy. Speaking and crying your struggles out into existence is giving your spirit permission to shed the parts of the past—the past meaning five seconds ago or five decades ago–that still grip your being. Please, be gentle. You deserve to nurture your soul.

The more we tap into our power, our knowing, our intuition, our subtle yet overwhelming gut feelings, the more we find what our souls are looking for.

You want to know how to trust your gut feeling is right? You listen. You respect yourself enough to trust your intuition. You get alone and you get quiet with your soul, and something within you will know. Don't doubt.

You are more powerful than you know. You have the power you need to make decisions that are aligned with your highest potential path. *Where do I even start?* You start by being alone with yourself and asking your soul what you need. You make the choice to work on yourself. No one can push you but you.

Your past is shedding away. Maybe you feel what you are feeling because you are ready for this transformation. Maybe you are ready to fully experience the uncomfortable emotions so that you can be freed. Maybe you feel like you are mourning your old life because where you are now isn't where you thought you would be. Maybe you are grieving your old self. When you experience something traumatic, it can feel like a part of you died right after. Even if you know you wouldn't be who you are today if what happened didn't happen, it's okay to mourn or miss who you were before. Being fully free from your past can take a lot of time, but it doesn't mean you won't be freed. The more you sit with yourself and feel, the more you will heal. You will never find the peace you so desperately need (and deserve) if you don't do the work. Crying is a gift that physically releases what you are holding onto. Don't become trapped within yourself. Let it out. It doesn't have to be all at once. The more you check in with yourself, the more you will become aware of yourself. You will slowly learn what you need at any given moment. You will slowly learn to trust your spirit guiding you. You will slowly break away from your past and be born again into who you've been created to be. You are made new. You are not broken; you are hurting, but you are whole.

When your heart is beating out of your chest and you feel sick from anxiety, I hope you remind yourself it will pass like it always does. I hope you remind yourself that you are stronger than its force. You have it within you to heal yourself. You have it within you to find the peace that passes all understanding. Maybe you know why you're experiencing it, or maybe you don't—either way, it's really hard. Give it permission to pass through you like a wave that will carry it all away. Give your emotions permission to pour out of you. Feel it so that you can let go of it. Breathe with it and watch it leave your body, mind, and spirit. Inhale the energy that you need, the energy that is only light and love, the energy that your soul is held in. Remember, just because you struggle with anxiety does not make you broken or weak or whatever negative word you convince yourself that you are. Anxiety is a lesson that can lead to wisdom. Your soul is filled with compassion. Take care of yourself, okay?

Healing is never as far as it feels, and healing never happens overnight. Give your healing the space it needs.

Even if it feels like everything is falling into pieces, I hope you trust that those pieces are fitting into the places they need to.

The pain of today will fade away. What hurts now won't hurt someday. That someday may feel far away, but I promise you, being okay is always closer than you may feel. I promise you, if you just try one more time, you will get to a place you cannot fathom right now–a place that leaves you speechless in tears because you realize the life you are living is purely a gift. You will realize that all of the pains of your yesterdays led you to heaven on earth–to the most beautiful life that you will never take for granted. You will meet people who touch your soul in a way you have never experienced before. You will meet people who hold you on your way to your highest potential. They will see something in you that you cannot see, and they will speak greatness over your existence. They will believe in you without envy. They will remind you of what you need to be reminded of daily. Hold on. They are finding you, and you will not always feel this alone or misunderstood. In the meantime, become everything you need for yourself. Step away for a moment and look at yourself. Not in the mirror, but in your soul. You are far more precious than you know. You are far more capable than you know. I hope you feel hope, even if it's only a little bit of hope. That hope is your spirit guiding you to the place you need to be. That hope is your spirit reminding you that you will exist without the darkness you live with now. Remember, try one more time and then one more time again. Take it slow. You are finding your way to a life unimaginable and breathtakingly beautiful.

Sometimes, the best people for you can't be those closest to you, and that is really hard to accept. But listen, you have to do what's best for you and your mental health. Life is far too delicate to surround yourself with negative energy. Negative people only create roadblocks on our paths to potential. Negative people place negative thoughts on you. They hold themselves back, and they hold you back with them. Energy is everything. As you grow and set boundaries, you will notice the way you think changes. You will notice you have more energy throughout the day. *It's important to know that it is not your responsibility to be the person everyone goes to.* It is not your responsibility to save anyone from their downward spiral. One of the bravest things you can do to change your life is step away from people you love but know are bringing you down more than up. Maybe it's temporary, or maybe it's forever; either way, it is necessary for your mental health. You don't have to feel guilty. You aren't a bad human being because of the walls you have to build to protect your soul. The truth is, it is never a selfish move to do what's best for you.

It won't always hurt.

Somehow, someday,
it will all work out.

When you don't feel like yourself and day after day your emotions remain the same, let go. Let go of the need to control it all. Let go of the expectations that tell you if you don't feel a certain way soon you won't be okay. Let go of the expectation to feel better right away. When we go through transformations, it feels incredibly uncomfortable to the point pushing it away feels like the only way to be okay. But listen, it's incredibly important to not ignore the discomfort. You don't want to look back on your life and realize you spent all of those years trapped because you didn't deal with what you needed to when your soul was crying out for you to, do you? Oftentimes, feelings our minds perceive as negative are actually little signs leading us to the right decisions. You cannot ignore the work that needs to be done. You must be here now with the discomfort. You must feel it to free it. It won't always make sense, no. But the more you acknowledge what's going on within you, the more you will grow into yourself. You will get to know yourself better than anyone could ever know you, and you will move forward with more awareness. You will slowly become more aware of how to move through what you go through. You will slowly begin to see your life-changing around you because when you change the way you think, you change the way you live. When you change the way you think, you change what you attract. Negative thoughts give birth to negative experiences and attract negative people. Positive thoughts awaken purpose and peace. Changing the way you think is a tedious process, but slowly you will begin to see your daily thoughts naturally change—one thought at a time. Forgive your mind when it's talking negatively and erase that energy with a kind thought. This healing and transformative season is eternally important. Don't ignore it.

This is your sign
to not ignore
what is calling you forth.
You know what you need to do.

Before anyone else, be
there for yourself.

It's okay if you haven't felt like yourself for several days. It doesn't mean you won't find your way back to feeling like yourself soon.

It's going to take some time to process everything that led up to this. It's going to feel confusing and overwhelming and terrifying, but you will sort through it in your heart's timing. We can't rush what we know deep within us we're not ready to face yet. There's a difference between being scared and feeling a soul instinct. Healing must be met with grace. Meet your healing with grace.

The pain of today
won't necessarily be
the same tomorrow.
Pain always passes.

The release.

You cannot ignore your emotions anymore. You have to re-lease them into existence so that you can exist unattached to your past. The longer you hold onto what no longer serves you, the more painful the release will be in the long run. You are emotionally strong enough now to deal with it all. Maybe you will feel worse at first because feeling and remember-ing are extremely uncomfortable, but that doesn't mean you won't feel the freedom you desperately need soon. I promise you will feel new soon. You will look back on these moments and be in awe of the growth and strength you embraced. One of the bravest things you can do for yourself is feel what is calling your name. Those feelings that don't feel okay are signs that you're holding onto something that you shouldn't be. Give your soul permission to let go. Give your soul permission to release any negative, painful, dark, unwanted emotion into the hands of the Universe. Holding onto your past will not lead you to a future you're in love with. Letting go will show you where you need to go. Letting go opens up your spirit to lead you to places beyond your imagination. Trust beyond what you can see. Let the release be slow if you need it to be–time really is a healer. Please, don't be hard on yourself if you can't handle it all right now. Even if you don't believe it because you are clouded by the pain deep within you, you know what's best for you. Listen. You are safe to process everything however you choose to. You deserve to believe in your soul's ability to heal.

Listen, you really will be okay. Whatever is happening that hurts and aches your entire being will entirely fade away. The part of you that feels everything so intensely isn't a part of you that you should push away. You don't have to apologize for your emotions. You don't have to hide what you're feeling. You don't have to go through it, hiding the most vulnerable parts of yourself away for no one to see. You have to release it so you can free it. Show up for yourself and show someone what you are truly experiencing within. Please, don't hold it back. It's going to be uncomfortable in the beginning, but the comfort you will find after is worth it. You are worth it. You are a fighter, and you must not forget that. Hope always comes when we open ourselves to the possibility that we really will be okay. A lot of the time, life can be really difficult. But you cannot forget the moments it has been really beautiful, and you cannot forget that some of your most beautiful experiences are finding you and are on the way. Listen, life really is too short and delicate. Walk away from the drama. Walk away from anything that doesn't make you the best possible version of yourself. Walk away from anything that makes you farther away from what feels like home—you are your home. You are your safe place. You can create space in your daily life that is full of love and joy and peace and anything that reminds you why being alive is a true gift. Don't invite anyone or anything into your life that only brings you farther away from the peace that you deserve. Don't lose yourself trying to save everyone else. You are the most important thing to focus on. I don't want you to look back on your life and regret not choosing yourself over anyone else. You will continue to choose people who aren't good for you if you don't choose yourself first. You will repeat patterns that shouldn't be repeated. You cannot become someone you love when you choose to ignore what you need to be okay. Let go of the guilt. Let go of the worry of hurting someone you love. Let go of anything that does not belong in your life. If it is not helping you be the best person you can be, let it go. What feels so big and intense right now will pass through you and be held in the gentle hands of the Universe. Surrender.

You're not always going to feel this weak. Your strength is coming. Everything you need is coming. What you are looking for is coming.

You don't have to be scared to wake up in the morning because you're afraid you'll feel the feelings you felt today. Tomorrow is new. Invite peace to move through and renew you. And if the feelings of today are still there tomorrow, I hope you know that it won't last forever. Things really will get better.

One more tomorrow.

Maybe tomorrow won't be better than today, or maybe it will. Choose to see it through because the stars are always there, even when covered in clouds–your strength and hope are too. No matter what happens, you will get through.

What is it you are holding on to that no longer needs to hold power within you? Sitting alone and asking yourself this question is really difficult–everything within us wants to run away from everything uncomfortable. You're not going to feel like your best self when you are running away from yourself and your truth. We can't be freed until we lead ourselves into discomfort. We can't figure out what is the best decision for us when we're looking for the answers everywhere other than within ourselves. We have to stop distracting ourselves from reality. There are going to be moments in your life where a wave of memories and emotions comes over you when you least expect it. There are going to be moments in your life where you think something in your past no longer affects you, but then something taps into the memory, and you realize there is still healing that needs to happen. When this arises, you cannot be hard on yourself. You have to give yourself the same grace and more that you would give the person you love most in this world. You are not weak even if you feel like you are breaking inside. You are not any less than the people you compare yourself to. It's important to remember that everyone is going through something.

I'm so sorry you're feeling the pain that you're feeling. I'm so sorry everything hurts so intensely that you feel like you don't want to be here. I'm so sorry you know what it feels like to be held in the hands of complete darkness. I'm so sorry you feel like no one understands what you're feeling. I have to remind you that it's going to be okay. It won't feel like this for much longer. You have to let it pass and let it out. Release it all. Don't feel guilty for any thought that crosses your mind. It is all valid. You have been dealing with so much. It's too much, I know. But listen, the light is never as far as it feels. It is with you even in the darkest of moments. It is holding you, and it wants you to survive this. You can survive this. It feels so heavy right now, but you will find freedom soon. You are strong enough now. You can handle this. It is okay to lean on other people to hold you when you can't hold yourself. It is okay to break. Sometimes we have to hit a breaking point and experience the meltdown fully so that we can fully heal and be set free from what is tearing us apart. Whatever you are worried about at this moment, remind yourself that whatever happens, you will still be okay. You don't have to handle it all on your own. You are allowed to set boundaries for yourself. You are not a bad person. You deserve to do what's best for you. We can't control a lot in this life, but it's important not to forget that there is a lot we can control. I hope you choose to give yourself permission to break and cry and try to get through this so that you can experience the incredible wonders of living. I hope you choose to keep living because the world truly wouldn't be the same without you. You are supposed to be here. You belong. You are so much more important than you feel.

Even when you feel the most alone, you are not alone.

You deserve to be forgiven, and you deserve to forgive yourself. You aren't a bad person. You haven't messed up too much. You are simply trying your best how you know best. The past is gone. It's going to be alright.

I know what it's like to feel like no one in the world understands what you experience within. I know what it's like to lay on the floor crying so hard no noise comes out. I know what it feels like to feel like you don't belong anywhere, and I know what it feels like to never feel at home anywhere. I know what it feels like to feel so much all at once that every part of you hurts, and holding yourself in the fetal position is the only way you feel a little bit safer. I know what it feels like to just want it all to end. The voices get so loud, and you just need silence. You get to a place where you are so exhausted from constantly not feeling okay that you just don't want to be here anymore, not because you want to leave but because you crave peace. The lies we hear in our minds can become so strong that you start to believe the most horrible thoughts. Listen, you don't have to be okay. You are allowed to give up for the day and do nothing but focus on yourself. Please, don't give up on yourself. Hold on to the truth that you won't feel this way forever. Hold on to the truth that you will get to a place where you feel more okay than not okay most days. I know how uncomfortable it is to feel disconnected from your body for weeks and still not feel like yourself. It's disorienting and terrifying. It's so important to find a safe space you can go to when you don't feel okay. I go to my bathtub and close the curtain because I feel safe, and slowly, the intensity of the emotions subside. I sit with myself and examine everything going on in my mind. I don't let judgment in, and I ask for guidance to show me the way through it. In the past, I would've let the darkness consume me completely, but now I know I am always stronger than it because I have shown myself several times that I can get through anything. In those dark moments, we have to remember that we got through difficult moments before; we will get through this one too. Yes, you will get through. It will pass.

You don't need to compare
your life to anyone else's.
You are special and worthy
of anything you don't
think you're worthy of.

If people can't love you
for who you are then they
aren't your people.

You deserve to have people in your life who make you feel special when you want to feel special the most, but you don't need other people to be the source of what makes you feel worthy, important, validated, or special. You need to be the first person in your life to make you feel special. You deserve to be there for yourself in the way you are there for everyone else. You deserve to treat yourself to something that makes you happy every day. You deserve to have a safe space in your home where you can go and fulfill yourself. You can rebuild yourself when you feel you are breaking, and I hope you know it is so brave of you to break down. Feelings aren't always the truth, but oftentimes they are our guides. Listen. Breathe deeply with yourself. Let go of the pressure you put on yourself to feel a certain way. Let go of the judgment you put on yourself to be different than you are. There are probably many times you've laid in bed crying because you feel like no one understands you—that is a sign that more people than you know actually do, even if you don't know them.

You deserve to take care of yourself every second of every day like you do for others. The way you feel so deeply, and you care so deeply is a true gift, but sometimes it can feel the opposite. Those of us who feel and care like this oftentimes feel the loneliest. It is not selfish to want someone else to make you feel special. It is not selfish to want other people to take care of you. It is not selfish to be sad when your expectations aren't met. Let yourself feel the hurt, but also let yourself feel the power of being everything you need for yourself. Once you learn to lean on yourself and your inner power, you won't be as disappointed when others don't meet your desires. It's slow learning, but it is one of the most important lessons we can learn in this life. Meet yourself where you're at right now. Speak to yourself the same way you speak to others. Trust your own wisdom. Celebrate yourself. You are more than enough for yourself. Read that again—you are more than enough for yourself.

When breathing becomes too difficult, and everything becomes too much, I hope you hold on to any strength you have left and remind yourself it won't be this way forever—stay. Stay for the days ahead that are filled with the best memories you've made yet. They are coming. I hope you speak up for yourself and use whatever strength you have left to be honest about your thoughts. More people than you know battle them. You are not losing your mind. You are hurting, and that is nothing to be ashamed of. It's so sad that so many of us feel shameful because of our dark thoughts. We have to talk about them to free them and to give other people permission to free their own. It's so easy to feel completely alone within the darkness, but more people than we know are living within it, too. Light is never as far as it feels. Light is here now because we are created from love and light, so it is with us in every moment, no matter how dark our world becomes. When you are terrified of your own thoughts, and you don't know what to do anymore, reach out. Reach out to someone because someone always cares, and it's a lie when we tell ourselves no one does. You deserve to keep breathing, and you deserve to be here. You deserve to be okay. You will be okay. You are never a burden.

I know you're just trying to be okay, and I am so proud of you.

When you don't feel okay after going a long time finally being okay, you don't have to be scared that it's going to be as bad as before. Even if it is as bad or worse, you're still going to be okay. You're still going to come out of this. Every setback can lead to growth and strength like you've never experienced before. But listen, you don't have to be strong right now. You are allowed to stay in bed if that's the only place you feel a little bit safer within yourself and a little bit more okay. You are allowed to step back if pushing yourself feels like too much to handle right now. You aren't failing at life if you can't be productive all of the time. You aren't failing as a person if you're not doing okay. You deserve to be fully honest about what you're feeling without judgment. I hope you stop putting so much pressure on yourself to feel a certain way. I hope you replace harsh words towards yourself with gentle words. You have to stop being so hard on yourself. You are trying your best. Sometimes the most productive thing we can do some days is to make sure we're okay and get through the day. The thoughts that tell you you're the only person going through this and that no one understands you are lies. The thoughts that tell you that you deserve to feel this way and you won't ever be okay are lies. If telling yourself it's going to be okay hurts more than it helps, then tell yourself this is awful. You don't have to know what you need right now. You are free to just be. You don't have to worry about offending anyone. You don't have to worry about anything other than just making sure you're okay. You deserve to be listened to. You deserve to be shown that you're not alone and you are so deeply cared about. It will pass. Let it pass. You should be so proud of yourself for not giving up on yourself, even when giving up feels like the only way to be okay. You are so brave for feeling. You are so brave for being. Trust.

What feels really heavy and overwhelming right now won't feel this way forever. Meet your emotions where they are at—you aren't overreacting if something is bothering you.

It's okay if you have to have a day or many where you stay inside and simply just let time pass by. I know life can be a lot sometimes, and I don't want you to feel guilty for needing to do what helps you survive. Remember, little steps.

You don't have to figure out what's best for you right now. You don't have to feel like yourself right now. You don't have to be someone you're not to make other people feel better.

When you're finally feeling okay after so long of not being okay, and the people around you are going through their own darkness that disturbs your peace, know that it's okay to back away from being the one everyone leans on. They will see the strength and success you have found and subconsciously think you have the answers they need but the truth is they will not find what they're looking for if they don't make the choice to. It takes a lot of people crashing into the deepest rock bottom they've been in to find their way out of the darkness. It takes a lot of people feeling utterly alone to look for the help they need. From personal experience, I've learned that sometimes it's the people we know the least who help us the most in the most difficult seasons of our lives. It's the people unattached to our past and who have done their own healing work who can give us the tools we need. So please, release the guilt of needing space from someone's struggles.

You don't have to be strong,
but I hope you know you are
always stronger than you feel.

It's okay to feel what you feel,
no matter what you are feeling.

Whatever it is you are holding on to that no longer serves you, give it permission to let go of you. You cannot move on when you are holding on.

Please, take care of your precious mind and body. Nothing in this world is more important than making sure you are okay. Whatever you are going through, you will get through.

When everything feels uncomfortable, and you cannot settle, remind yourself that it will pass. Remind yourself that your past isn't who you are now and that who you are now isn't who you'll be forever–there is always room for growth. Your best is more than enough right now and always.

You are going through significant changes in your life, and anything you feel during this transition is valid. There is nothing wrong with you because you need to lean on others. You deserve to be supported just as much and more as you support others.

you are so much stronger
than you feel right now
the worries will soften away
and all will be okay

You have the power to be everything you need, and everything you need you can find within yourself, but, listen, you can be everything and still need to lean on others for support. You deserve to be held. You deserve to be listened to and nurtured. Give other people permission to support you. You are not weak; you are stronger than you'll ever know.

I know you're trying your absolute hardest to be okay. I know it's uncomfortable and terribly frustrating to be doing all of the work they suggest you do to be okay, and nothing seems to help. But listen, just because it feels like nothing is helping, sometimes growth and healing happen the deepest when we aren't consciously aware of it. You are finding whole healing. Give yourself all of the time you need–maybe it feels like a rush, but there is no rush.

You are seen. You are being
held through the discomfort no
matter how lonely it becomes.

When your heart is sitting locked up in your chest, making it difficult to breathe, I hope you know you will find the peace you need soon. It's okay to let go of the pressure you are putting on yourself to be feeling something you are not.

It may seem like you're the only one feeling these feelings; it may get so lonely to the point you think you're going crazy because you don't have anyone to relate to, but I promise you, you are not the only one going through it. All of your feelings are valid.

Good times are on their way.

You can do even the most
difficult things.

Be there for yourself before anyone else. Do whatever you have to do. Listen to what your body needs. Listen to what your soul needs.

You should be so proud of yourself for how hard you are try-ing and have always tried. You should be so proud of yourself for trying to take care of yourself even though it feels like it's leading you nowhere. Maybe sometimes you think to yourself it would just be easier to give up now rather than continue to struggle through it all, but I know there is a piece of you that knows giving up isn't the right thing to do.

You are going to come through this stronger and wiser. You are going to come through this with more tools and understanding of life than most people do in their entire lifetime.

You have been called to this path. You have been chosen to learn these lessons now because your soul knows you are going to do something good with it.

You are someone who takes pain and turns it into a gain of strength. There are people who are okay today because of you—because you chose to show up to the pain and do something with it. Not everyone would do what you have done with what you have been dealt. Not everyone would choose to show up to this healing every day the way you are.

What you are going through is temporary.

What feels never-ending will end. What hurts now will find healing. What doesn't make sense may never make sense, but this doesn't mean you will never find peace with it. The peace you are seeking is not as far away as it feels. Even if it feels like no one understands how hard you are trying to simply be okay by the end of the day, you know, and that can be enough.

Validation from others will never satisfy your soul the way you need–only you can give yourself the fulfillment you need. At the end of the day, we only have ourselves. We know ourselves the best. We live within our minds our whole lives; we can't expect anyone else to fully understand us. I hope you find time every day to get to know yourself a little bit better.

You are going to look back on these times with tears in your eyes and think, "This is how it needed to be." Maybe it didn't all happen how you deserved or would have chosen, but it made you choose yourself. It made you become the person you are today, and that is a power nothing and no one can take away from you.

Maybe you feel deep within you that you aren't where you are supposed to be right now, but maybe you actually are. Maybe you are being held in this place so that you can grow and heal before you go somewhere else. Maybe you are being protected. Maybe you are being given a rare opportunity to focus on yourself and no one else for a while. It might feel uncomfortable and lonely, but maybe these feelings aren't negative. Maybe it is in these moments you discover yourself in a way that helps you change for the better. Maybe you will carry the lessons you learn now with you forever. You see, it is in the seasons that make the least sense we grow the most. It is in the seasons that are the most uncomfortable that we become more comfortable with ourselves. I hope you lean into these moments with surrender. Surrender to the journey your soul is on. You are always being guided to where you belong. Even if you don't feel like you belong where you are right now, you won't stay in this place forever. Before you know it, the dreams you are dreaming of now will be your reality when they are supposed to be. Trust.

It's okay if your heart needs
more time than your mind
does to accept what you know
deep within you to be true.

You should be so proud of yourself for walking away from situations in order to put yourself first. I know it's not easy to separate yourself from anything that at one time or another felt good or right or comfortable. I promise, if you haven't seen the benefits fully yet, you will soon.

You deserve rest if you need rest.

Give yourself permission to
do what's best for you.

Your past doesn't have to hurt your future. Your past doesn't have to tell you how to feel. Your past doesn't have to be something that makes today miserable. You deserve to be renewed. You deserve to live in freedom from the pain the past has held you in for too long.

I hope you know that your worth
should never be a reflection of
someone else's opinions.

Now is the time to stop believing you deserve anything less than the best. There will be people who treat you better than you have ever been treated. Hold on, they'll find you.

Day to day, progress looks different. Progress is still progress, even if there is no one besides you who sees it. Let your recognition be enough because it is.

I just hope that no matter how hard it gets, you don't stop being yourself. Life is too short to not love yourself for exactly who you are.

You matter so much more than
you think. You belong even
when you don't feel like it.

Everything you need is never as far as it seems. These difficult times now will one day soon be a memory of a time in your life you overcame something you didn't think you could. Your courage and strength stretch far into your future. You will make it.

I know you're tired and didn't ask to be handed the life that you have been. Maybe you were chosen for this journey because your story is going to help heal someone else–you may be the someone for someone else that you needed but never had. Maybe you were chosen for this journey because you're the one that is strong enough to handle the heaviness of it all. *I'm sorry it's been hard, but I'm proud of you for making it through.*

I hope you know the world is
better because you exist in it.

Even after all of the letdowns, you took a chance, and that is something you should be so proud of. You tried. Even if it doesn't work out, you tried, and that's more than enough.

As alone as you feel right now, this is your reminder that you are not alone.

Here's to the small moments. The moments that may seem insignificant now, but those we'll look back on and know we wouldn't be who we are without them. Small steps. Your life doesn't need to come together all at once.

Your time on this earth isn't over. You are going to feel the sunshine you have so desperately needed. This earth needs you.

You are still standing. After everything you have been through, you have made it through. Please, don't forget this because you will make it through it all. You will.

As you are, it is enough. You are enough even when the world and your thoughts make you compare yourself to everything and everyone.

One breath at a time.

If taking it one day at a time feels like
too much, take it one breath at a time.
You are allowed to slow down.

No matter what,
in the end,
you will be okay.

Your way of
feeling so deeply
is your soft strength.

Love without losing yourself. Don't give too much of your-self to someone that you don't have enough left to give to yourself. You deserve to be loved deeply, if your love isn't being returned, remind yourself that you deserve better.

You deserve the kind of love that heals the parts of you that you thought could never be healed.

It is time to start taking care of yourself more than you take care of others. Sometimes it is easier to distract our own healing with the struggles others are going through, but you will never be the person you have the potential to be if you don't work through your personal struggles. It's okay to not know where to start or have the energy to start—you take it one breath at a time, one little action forward at a time, one moment of grace and power at a time.

I hope you learn to stop judging yourself–you are doing the best you can with what you've been given. Learning to be kinder to yourself will never be met with the negative chatter your mind wraps you in too much of the time. Over time, as you do the work, you will learn how to soften those thoughts. Feeling and thinking deeply can become your soft power. The way you experience this life so deeply can lead you to places that those who don't let themselves feel never get to, places that are more beautiful and fulfilling than you can even imagine. I hope you trust your journey in feeling.

Never feel guilty for doing
what's best for you.

You saved yourself. No one else did. It was always you.

Listen, I know it's scary and uncomfortable and deeply upsetting right now, but you are going to be okay. You have to take this step for yourself. You have to reach beyond what is known and try to trust that you will be okay no matter what. Even if it doesn't work out. Even if you don't find what you're looking for, it's honorable to show yourself that you tried. It is admirable to get help. You are not weak. You are not worthless. You are not a failure. No one will be upset with you for doing what you need to do for you. Your light is stronger than any darkness. Remember, the courage you need is already within you. The comfort you need is already within you. You can do whatever you think you can't do.

If you're holding the weight of someone else's world on your shoulders, no matter who that person is to you, and somewhere within you, you know it's not your weight to hold, give yourself permission to let go. It doesn't have to be your responsibility all of the time. It doesn't always have to be you being the glue for everyone all of the time. Sometimes loving someone looks like letting go and letting them figure out the path they need to take. Maybe you will look back on these times and see that you needed to let go so they could move forward. I know it's not easy or simple. I know when you love someone all you want to do is take all of their struggles away, but you have to remember that sometimes people grow the most through the hardest times. Maybe this struggle is what they need in order to change and heal parts of them you don't even know they need healed. When it becomes too much, you have to trust that they will be okay and you should never feel guilty for putting yourself first.

You deserve to wholeheartedly love yourself and your life. You deserve to break free from your past and the hurt it has held you in for too long. You deserve to find whole healing and full freedom from any darkness that tries to take your light. You deserve to finally find the peace your soul has been searching for. You deserve to see yourself as someone who is beautiful—you wouldn't be here if you weren't meant to be precisely the person you are. You deserve to be loved by someone who loves you with unconditional love—the kind of love you have always dreamed of. I hope you never tell yourself that you are worth nothing because you are worth everything. Sometimes life is beautiful and then unimaginably difficult, but that doesn't mean it won't be beautiful again. You can't wait until life doesn't hurt anymore to choose to believe you deserve more. You can't wait until you feel ready to start stepping toward your dreams. You deserve to find everything you're looking to get out of this precious life. More than anything I just hope you know that you deserve to be here, now. The world would never be the same without you.

For the one who needs to know that things will get better...

Listen, things really will get better. It won't happen right away, but that doesn't mean you won't be okay sooner than it feels like. When your heart is being held in a realm of darkness and it feels like the struggles are becoming too much, it's difficult to see any light of hope. It's difficult to hear any encouragement or positivity because it's all just so exhausting. The more you remind yourself that it will get better, the closer to a better reality you will get. Too often, we get in the way of our healing just by the way we talk to ourselves. You will find yourself looking back on these days, feeling grateful you made it through, feeling grateful for the way you grew through it all. Finding patience in the process of being okay again starts with giving yourself as much time and grace as you need. It starts with reminding yourself there is no rush. Your healing is happening in your timing. It's normal to need a break from it, but there will come a time when you just have to go for it. And you will be ready.

The strength that you gain
from the pain you survive will
become your strongest power.

You are going to have days where you can barely get out of bed. You are also going to have days that you don't want to end. No matter what happens day to day, be really gentle with the way your body and mind are processing life. Listen to what your body is telling you and please don't feel guilty if you need to slow down for more than a day or two. You deserve as many moments as you need for yourself to reset, even if it's just one deep breath.

This uncomfortable moment will pass, just as every uncomfortable moment has passed before.

Whatever thoughts are making it feel difficult to breathe, let them come and go without judgment. Let go of the impulsion to judge yourself for feeling how you feel. Let go of the desire to know how the unknown will play out. Let go of anything holding you back from being present, in this exact moment, from simply existing in the now. Just as your eyes pass by one word at a time in a book, let your life write its story one breath at a time, one experience at a time, one second at a time. Whatever feels too much right now, will sometime soon be a memory. A memory of a moment you got through. Instead of sitting in the negative, you can instead do something with it. You can sit with your mind and observe the experience. You can see how maybe it's an opportunity for necessary growth. Or maybe it's an opportunity to show yourself you can get through it on your own. There are endless, eternal, lessons that can be learned within the uncomfortable times. Let the future live in the future. Let the story be written as it intends to. Let yourself be guided. You are becoming everything you've needed to be. Maybe not how you thought it would all happen. Maybe not in a way you would have chosen, but maybe, just maybe, you were chosen to become this story for a reason. Maybe you were the only one who could handle it and do with it what you are. You should be so proud of the way you've made your way through.

What do you do when you feel stuck and have no energy? You start by taking a gentle step back and notice how you are talking to yourself. You remind yourself that it is okay to not know what you need right now. It is okay to feel so frustrated to the point where you need to take a break from thinking deeply for some time. When you are ready, you have to come back from the break and meet yourself where you are at. You cannot keep ignoring your feelings. You cannot keep putting off your moving forward. Other people can help give you ideas or suggestions, but ultimately it is up to you to choose which path you take. Trust your deep, sometimes very subtle instincts. You are energy. The truth is, you can choose what you allow to bring you down or bring you up. Remember, setting boundaries with the people around you is never selfish. This is your reminder that you have to start choosing yourself as the number one priority in your life.

Please, just keep pushing through. Something new and better than you could ever dream of is coming to you.

You are not broken because you weren't chosen by the one you so desperately wish chose you.

I know when you're going through something difficult, the last thing you want to hear is encouragement. I know it's nearly impossible to think positive when everything has been negative for too long. In those moments, know that it's okay to close the book. It's okay to turn off the optimism. It's okay to just sit there and distract yourself. Sometimes our minds simply need silence for some time. But I hope you don't forget to come back when you are ready and try to fill yourself with something good, with something that reminds you of the hope that you're forgetting is near because hope is always here. Remind yourself of a good memory. Remind yourself that even if you don't feel ready to heal, you are always more capable than you feel. You really are always doing better than you think you are.

Rest isn't rest if you're being hard on yourself for resting. Feeling guilty for not feeling motivated or productive will only drain you more. You're probably tired because when you take a break you're not actually taking a break. Lean in to doing nothing and start taking care of yourself however that looks for you. Stop judging yourself. Be kinder, you've accomplished more than you give yourself credit for.

You've been through so much already. You deserve for your life to move forward for the better. Even if it gets difficult, *it always gets better*.

You are healing here. No matter how far away from being healed you feel you are, you are still healing and that is just as important as being healed.

You are stronger than you
feel and braver than what
tries to bring you down.

Not only will it get better, but
it will be better than you ever
dreamed it could be.
Claim this now.

If you can slowly start to learn and practice being kinder to yourself, your whole world will change. A little more kindness a day goes a long way.

It's time to stop getting in your own way and it's time to start living in a way that, a little bit each day, you begin to become who you know you are capable of becoming. It's hard enough when circumstances out of our control interrupt our paths, sometimes it's just as difficult to look back and know we could've made a change sooner if we trusted ourselves. This is your sign to do what you know you need to do in order to improve your life—even if you're doubting, even if it pushes people away, even if it's not the easy way to go from here. At least give yourself the chance to try. You deserve for things to go up from here.

When you feel like you haven't felt like yourself for a while and it becomes deeply upsetting, let yourself feel deeply upset about it. Your depth of feeling isn't a weakness. Your depth of feeling will actually lead you to a more fulfilling life experience. So let yourself feel the strangeness of the disconnect. Let yourself feel how frustrating it is to have one thing after another be uncomfortable. You shouldn't force yourself to feel something you're not. You shouldn't force yourself to do anything you don't feel well enough to do. Sometimes the best thing you can do for your body is just be. In the same way, you don't want fear to hold you back, you shouldn't let comparison make you do anything that doesn't feel authentic to you.

Choosing to take care of yourself is never the easy thing to do. There's nothing simple about slowing down and ignoring the pressures of the world. There's nothing simple about choosing to put yourself first for the sake of your sanity when you're living in a world that shows the highlights of people's lives right in front of you more than the low lights are seen. Everyone is always going through something even if they don't show it.

It's in the low points we discover our light the most. It's in the low points we discover the power of our strength the most. It's in the low point we grow the most and are prepared for the next thing. We're always more ready for the next thing than we think we are. When you are someone that has experienced so many low points, the high points are always higher, because gratitude comes alive more.

All of this worrying about the unknown won't lead you to where you want to be. So please, slow down. Give yourself a chance to breathe without putting pressure on yourself. Quiet the to-do list. What needs to get done will get done when you can. It's okay if you can't do it all today or within a year. Your life is unfolding and you are going to get done what you need to get done in your life.

I hope you don't forget that you are
stronger than you were and it's because
you chose strength over brokenness.
Courage over comfort. Faith over fear.

We always end up back with the people we're meant to–even if a long time goes by, the soul friends are always there, no matter what.

You are going to realize someday
that all of this isn't for nothing.
You are being built, not broken.

And maybe you didn't choose this path but maybe this path chose you for a reason that someday you will be able to understand and actually be grateful for. But even if you don't feel any gratitude in the end, that's okay too.

JACQUELINE WHITNEY is a writer from Philadelphia, Pennsylvania. Her words are a daily source of comfort for many.

instagram.com/jacquelinewhitney_
tiktok.com/@jacquelinewhitney_

Printed in Great Britain
by Amazon